The Life of
Rosa Parks

By Kathleen Connors

Gareth Stevens
Publishing

Please visit our website, www.garethstevens.com. For a free color catalog of all our high-quality books, call toll free 1-800-542-2595 or fax 1-877-542-2596.

Library of Congress Cataloging-in-Publication Data

Connors, Kathleen.
The Life of Rosa Parks / by Kathleen Connors.
  p. cm. — (Famous lives)
Includes index.
ISBN 978-1-4824-0422-7 (pbk.)
ISBN 978-1-4824-0423-4 (6-pack)
ISBN 978-1-4824-0419-7 (library binding)
1. Parks, Rosa, — 1913-2005 — Juvenile literature. 2. African American women — Alabama — Montgomery — Biography — Juvenile literature. 3. African Americans — Alabama — Montgomery — Biography — Juvenile literature. I. Connors, Kathleen. II. Title.
F334.M753 C66 2014
323.092—dc23

First Edition

Published in 2014 by
Gareth Stevens Publishing
111 East 14th Street, Suite 349
New York, NY 10003

Copyright © 2014 Gareth Stevens Publishing

Designer: Nicholas Domiano
Editor: Kristen Rajczak

Photo credits: Cover, p. 1 the US Postal Service via Getty Images; pp. 5, 7 Photo12/UIG/Getty Images; p. 9 Don Cravens/Time & Life Pictures/Getty Images; p. 11 Underwood Archives/Archive Photos/Getty Images; pp. 13, 15 Grey Villet/Time & Life Pictures/Getty Images; p. 17 William Philpott/Getty Images News/Getty Images; p. 19 Paul Sancya/AFP/Getty Images; p. 21 MCT/McClatchy-Tribune/Getty Images.

Printed in the United States of America

CPSIA compliance information: Batch #CW14GS: For further information contact Gareth Stevens, New York, New York at 1-800-542-2595.

Contents

Boldface words appear in the glossary.

Quiet Beginnings

When Rosa Louise McCauley was born in 1913, no one knew she'd make a stand for **civil rights**! Rosa lived on her grandparents' farm in Alabama. She went to a **segregated** school where her mother taught.

5

Rosa had to leave school to care for her grandmother and mother when they became ill. But after she married Raymond Parks in 1932, she was able to go back. Rosa was proud of her high school **diploma**!

7

Equality for All

Rosa and Raymond believed everyone should be equal. They joined the **NAACP** in Montgomery, Alabama, hoping to help blacks gain their civil rights. Rosa worked as a secretary for the group.

Making a Stand

In 1955, Rosa boarded a bus after work in Montgomery. At the time, there was a law that said a black person had to give up their seat if a white person needed it. Rosa refused! She was **arrested**.

On the day of Rosa's trial, black leaders planned a **boycott** of all the city buses in Montgomery, Alabama. It was a big statement because many blacks used buses to get around.

Rosa was fined, but she wouldn't pay. By 1956, her case had reached the US **Supreme Court**. It declared Alabama's segregation laws illegal! This decision ended the bus boycott after 381 days.

Forward Motion

Rosa's troubles weren't over. She lost her job. Some people said they wanted to hurt her. She and her family then moved to Detroit, Michigan, in 1957. None of this stopped Rosa from believing in equality!

17

Rosa's continued support of the civil rights movement earned her great praise. In 1996, she was given the Presidential Medal of Freedom. Then, Rosa received the Congressional Gold Medal in 1999.

Her Story Lives On

Rosa died in 2005. Today, she's often called the "mother of the civil rights movement." Rosa's story teaches a very important lesson—even small actions can have a big impact!

Timeline

1913 — Rosa is born.

1932 — Rosa marries Raymond Parks.

1955 — Rosa won't give up her bus seat. She's arrested.

1956 — The Supreme Court rules that bus segregation is illegal.

1996 — Rosa receives the Presidential Medal of Freedom.

2005 — Rosa dies at age 92.

Glossary

arrest: to take charge of someone by law

boycott: the act of refusing to have dealings with a person or business in order to force change

civil rights: the freedoms granted to us by law

diploma: a piece of writing that states completion of something, such as schooling

NAACP: the National Association for the Advancement of Colored People, a civil rights organization founded in 1909

segregate: to forcibly separate races or classes

Supreme Court: the highest court in the United States

For More Information

Books

Edison, Erin. *Rosa Parks*. North Mankato, MN: Capstone Press, 2013.

Waldman, Neil. *A Land of Big Dreamers: Voices of Courage in America*. Minneapolis, MN: Millbrook Press, 2010.

Websites

Notable Civil Rights Leaders

www.factmonster.com/spot/bhmpeople2.html

Learn about many more leaders of the civil rights movement.

Rosa Parks

www.ducksters.com/biography/women_leaders/rosa_parks.php

Read about Rosa Parks's life, and use links to discover other important people in history.

Index